LIVING HOPE

A DEVOTIONAL FOR THE CHURCH, BY THE CHURCH

A NOTE FROM SENIOR PASTOR JACK GRAHAM

As we make our way toward Holy Week, let us truly prepare our hearts for Easter and the Resurrection of our Lord and Savior.

Make sure that you engage daily in this five-week journey that will help strengthen your soul, your heart and your mind, resting assured that your hope is found in Christ.

Because Jesus lives, we have a future and a hope with Him! He has delivered and conquered death! And therefore, we live in hope!

Now hope, of course, is essential for life. You wouldn't live very long in hopelessness. It's a lifeline. What oxygen is to the lungs, hope is to the soul. The Bible tells us that hope is an anchor for the soul. What an anchor is to a ship, hope is to the soul.

An anchor provides security and steadiness in the midst of a storm. That's what hope is. Hope is the certainty that because of the Resurrection, our future as believers is in His hands. And because of Easter, because Jesus is alive, we have this incredible hope and future.

Whatever you may be struggling with or living with in these days, please take time to meditate on God's Word and commit to this journey toward the Cross with us. Trust in our Savior who is alive! Our hope is in Christ and Christ alone!

In Christ alone,

Jack Graham

HOW TO USE THIS BOOK

Within this book, you will take a five-week journey, front and center, into the powerful story of the Crucifixion and Resurrection of Jesus Christ – our "living hope." The first four weeks of the book will strengthen your heart, soul and mind by working through a different spiritual discipline each week. Those disciplines will then set the table for week five, Holy Week. Our goal in writing this is to come alongside you and help you put your faith into practice, preparing your heart for the powerful story displayed throughout Holy Week. Within the pages of this book, your days will consist of either a "Daily Devotional" or a "Faith in Practice." Below, you will find a description on how to navigate those.

DAILY DEVOTIONALS

SCRIPTURE You will find Scripture within each day of the readings. Take time to read and meditate on the Word.

RESPONSE You will be challenged and asked to respond to what is being taught through the questions within each devotional.

PRAYER Prayer has the incredible ability to draw us close to God while making us more like Jesus. You will find a section within each devotional to write your daily prayer to God.

MUSIC You will find music interwoven throughout the book that brings a beautiful parallel for you while you read. Scan the QR code at the start of every chapter to find a playlist specifically chosen for that week's theme.

FAITH IN PRACTICE On these days, you will be asked to put your faith into practice in a variety of ways. Our goal with these inserts is to help you practice the spiritual disciplines you are walking through and push your devotional time to the next level. We believe a key to full devotion to Jesus is consistent, intentional and deep devotion in the secret place. We pray you find these times to be fruitful for your walk with Jesus.

For additional resources and to learn more about our church, please visit prestonwood.org.

contents

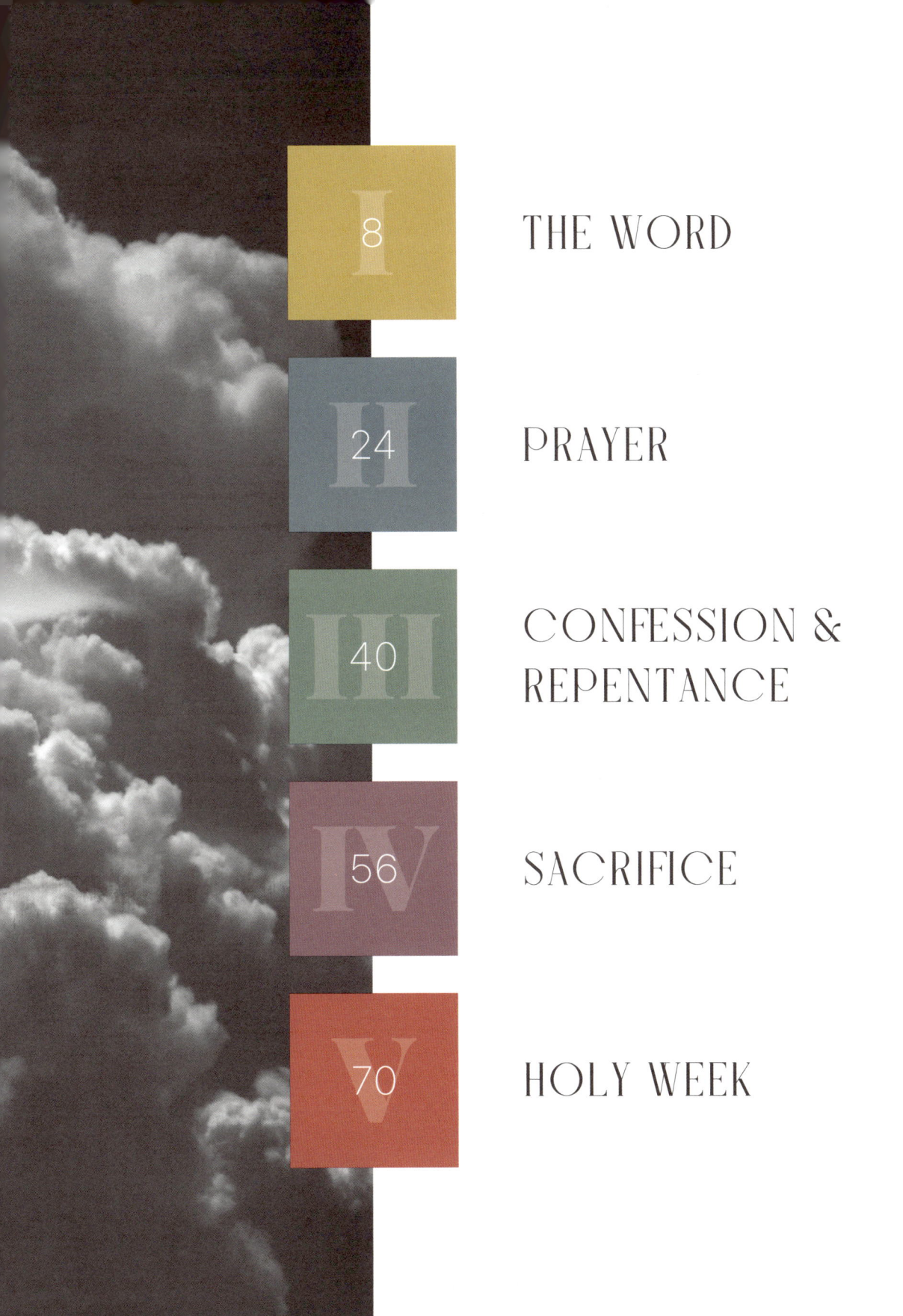

I	8	THE WORD
II	24	PRAYER
III	40	CONFESSION & REPENTANCE
IV	56	SACRIFICE
V	70	HOLY WEEK

I

THE WORD

All Scripture is breathed out by God and profitable for teaching, for reproof, for correction, and for training in righteousness, that the man of God may be complete, equipped for every good work.

2 TIMOTHY 3:16-17

There is great power in the Word of God. We are blessed with the ability to access it anytime we wish. As we walk through this section, we will be reminded of the true depth of His Word.

DAY 1

AN AUTHORITATIVE WORD

All Scripture is breathed out by God and profitable for teaching, for reproof, for correction, and for training in righteousness, that the man of God may be complete, equipped for every good work.

2 TIMOTHY 3:16-17

God is not man, that he should lie, or a son of man, that he should change his mind. Has he said, and will he not do it? Or has he spoken, and will he not fulfill it?

NUMBERS 23:19

"Sword of the Spirit," "Scriptures," "Word of God" – These are a few titles one might use when referring to the Bible.

However, has our use and view of the Bible shrunk? Has it become a book of text used only when prompted? Or do we consider it to be the very way that God intended to communicate with His children?

Second Timothy 3:16 says that *all* Scripture is breathed out by God; we also know the Bible was written by more than 40 authors across a span of 1,600 years. These authors had different occupations, personalities and interests, and the fact that all 66 books seamlessly showcase the Gospel allows us a glimpse of God's sovereignty. One could compare this miracle to Jesus Christ being both fully man and fully God – how could it be?

Trying to wrap one's mind around this process can be difficult, and it can cause some to view Scripture as a suggestive, therapy-based book. However, there are severe consequences to this view. If we were to start picking and choosing verses that only apply to us and agree with our own personal views, we limit the teaching, reproofing, correcting and training that 2 Timothy 3:17 argues is necessary for us to be "complete, equipped for every good work."

As North Campus Pastor Connor Bales says, the Bible is written for "personal transformation, not informational dissemination."

Numbers 23:19 makes it clear that God's character is both unchanging and constant; therefore, since all Scripture is breathed out by God, every word is consistent and worthy of our attention. Its reliability and inspiration make it authoritative for us as followers of Christ, and we can trust that every word is profitable for teaching and correcting – even the ones that make us uncomfortable!

> **How does the idea of the Bible's authority over our lives change the way you read it, and the ways you can dig deeper into Scripture?**

SONG FOR TODAY

"AUTHORITY"

Elevation Worship

DAY 2

#GOALS

All Scripture is breathed out by God and profitable for teaching, for reproof, for correction, and for training in righteousness, that the man of God may be complete, equipped for every good work.

2 TIMOTHY 3:16-17

For the word of God is living and active, sharper than any two-edged sword, piercing to the division of soul and of spirit, of joints and of marrow, and discerning the thoughts and intentions of the heart.

HEBREWS 4:12

Who doesn't love a good underdog story? You know, those movies where the main character is struggling and having a really hard time in the beginning, but then, throughout the course of the movie, transforms into the hero? That character had goals to achieve, hoops to jump through, and a lot had to happen in this character's life to become that hero. Let's pause right here and take a moment to read Hebrews 4:12.

You may be thinking, "What in the world? ... A sword divides my soul and spirit?!" Hebrews 4:12 is referring to Scripture, the Bible, God's holy Word. God's Word had many writers but there is only *one* author: The Holy Spirit.

God's Word changes us when we spend time meditating and memorizing it. Now let's read 2 Timothy 3:16–17 again.

God's Word is infallible, which means it is incapable of making mistakes or being wrong. If all Scripture is inspired by God, that means that *all of it* is incapable of making mistakes or being wrong. Since this is true, the second part of this verse is also true.... It is useful for teaching, rebuking and correcting. Circle back to the story that we all love about the underdog. Heroes go through trials, moments that teach them, and people who correct them; and they train to prepare themselves to become the person we see at the end of the movie. The person who is a better version than before. That's what God does with us through His Word. When we spend time memorizing His Word, reading His Word, and meditating on His Word, the Holy Spirit transforms us to become more like Him. Scripture leads us to our righteousness (free of guilt and sin) in and through Christ. Hebrews 4:12 says, "For the word of God is living and active, sharper than any two-edged sword, piercing to the division of soul and of spirit, of joints and of marrow, and discerning the thoughts and intentions of the heart." The #GOAL of our life is to follow after Jesus with our whole heart and allow Him to transform our heart, soul and mind through His righteousness which is achieved by our spending time with Him in His Word.

How will you allow God's Word to transform your life today? Think of at least two different ways you can actively pursue this throughout the next 24 hours.

SONG FOR TODAY

"COME THOU FOUNT OF EVERY BLESSING"

Come Thou fount of every blessing
Tune my heart to sing Thy grace
Streams of mercy never ceasing
Call for songs of loudest praise

FAITH IN

MEDITATE

MEDITATE

PRACTICE

DAY 3

Meditating on God's Word actively grows our faith, giving us the ability to apply it to our lives. This spiritual practice will allow the Word of God to invade even the deepest part of our hearts. When the Word of God is deep within our heart, we will see our faith strengthen. Sit, be still, and meditate on His Word.

PSALM 1:1-6

Blessed is the man
who walks not in the counsel of the wicked,
nor stands in the way of sinners,
nor sits in the seat of scoffers;
but his delight is in the law of the LORD,
and on his law he meditates day and night.
He is like a tree
planted by streams of water
that yields its fruit in its season,
and its leaf does not wither.
In all that he does, he prospers.
The wicked are not so,
but are like chaff that the wind drives away.
Therefore the wicked will not stand in the judgment,
nor sinners in the congregation of the righteous;
for the LORD knows the way of the righteous,
but the way of the wicked will perish.

Scan the QR code to experience the fullness of these devotionals by listening to the worship songs complementing them.

DAY 4

WE'RE ALL TEACHING SOMETHING

All Scripture is breathed out by God and profitable for teaching, for reproof, for correction, and for training in righteousness....

2 TIMOTHY 3:16

For the word of God is living and active, sharper than any two-edged sword, piercing to the division of soul and of spirit, of joints and of marrow, and discerning the thoughts and intentions of the heart.

HEBREWS 4:12

Teachers hold a special place in our hearts. We remember them for various reasons. Some we fell in love with and wanted to be in their classes for the rest of our lives. Some we counted down the days until we moved to the next grade or class. Take a moment to think about your favorite teachers in school. What made them your favorite? Was it how they taught the content? Was it their personality and attitude? Was it their smile as you entered the classroom each day? Perhaps it was the warmth their classroom gave?

We have all liked former teachers for various reasons, but the fact is, they were all teachers. They all taught us different subjects and imparted knowledge on us every day. These subjects were vital to learn as we grow older and work toward degrees and careers.

In the previous devotional, we saw that Scripture is profitable, leads us to righteousness, and is useful for teaching. The Word of God speaks to and teaches on many different topics. It teaches us about love (1 Corinthians 13), friendship

(1 John), marriage (Ephesians 5), loneliness (Psalm 88), wealth (James 5:1–6), and worry (Matthew 6:25–34), to name just a few. So, if Scripture teaches us, why shouldn't we use it to teach *others*?

God's Word addresses all the topics we will encounter in life and shines an incredible light on them. See Hebrews 4:12 on the previous page. It calls God's Word "sharp" and illustrates it as having the ability to pierce our heart, soul and spirit. There is no other book on the face of the planet with this kind of power. There is no other written word anywhere that can teach us that way. If it has this kind of power, why wouldn't we use it to teach others?

The fact is, we must use God's Word to teach those around us. To hold on to God's Word and keep it for ourselves is the exact opposite of its intention. God gave us this book to share with everyone. He gave it to us to teach and leave a legacy for all the generations that would come.

But how will they know if we aren't willing to tell them? How can we teach others if we aren't allowing God's Word to teach us? If God's Word is truly one that is breathed out by our holy, Creator God and is profitable in many ways, then why aren't we teaching those around us?

What or how does God's Word need to teach you today so that you can teach God's Word to those around you?

SONG FOR TODAY

"LORD, I NEED YOU"
Matt Maher

DAY 5

GOD'S WORD CORRECTS US

All Scripture is breathed out by God and profitable for teaching, for reproof, for correction, and for training in righteousness....

2 TIMOTHY 3:16

For the word of God is living and active, sharper than any two-edged sword, piercing to the division of soul and of spirit, of joints and of marrow, and discerning the thoughts and intentions of the heart.

HEBREWS 4:12

... so shall my word be that goes out from my mouth; it shall not return to me empty, but it shall accomplish that which I purpose, and shall succeed in the thing for which I sent it.

ISAIAH 55:11

Correction, whether given with ease or with force, is not something most people generally receive well. However, correction comes out of an overflow of love from a caring authority figure. This could be a parent, a grandparent, a stepparent, etc. This is no different when it comes to God's Word correcting our life and ensuring that the reader is walking in the freedom that only He offers (John 10:10).

Spending time in God's Word is not simply something we do to check off a spiritual to-do list, but something we do because a loving Father has written His instructions for holy living in a 66-book-long love letter. In this love letter, God counters man's inclination to completely forget what He has done, is doing, and promised He will do – because it doesn't fit into what we think is best. This is where there must be a shift in the how we view God's

Word. It is not only a place to go when comfort is needed, but also a place to go and see where our life doesn't match up to what He's called us to (Psalm 139:23–24).

Like David in Psalm 139, we cry out, begging God to search us and reveal to us our deficiencies and the ability to submit to His Word in correcting those areas. And we can pray knowing that His Word will not return empty.

> **Is there something in your life the Lord is trying to correct with His Word? How have you responded to that correction?**

SONG FOR TODAY

"PSALM 139 (FAR TOO WONDERFUL)"
Shane & Shane

DAY 6

TRAINING IN RIGHTEOUSNESS

All Scripture is breathed out by God and profitable for teaching, for reproof, for correction, and for training in righteousness, that the man of God may be complete, equipped for every good work.

2 TIMOTHY 3:16-17

Perhaps at some point, you completed a formal season of education, whether a high school diploma, college degree or post-graduate degree(s). Nevertheless, while the paper signifying your achievement might be on the wall, as a disciple of Jesus, you've never graduated from being a lifelong learner.

As disciples of Jesus and being people of the Bible, we must entrench and immerse ourselves in the Bible. It's in God's Word that we find spiritual nourishment and kingdom instruction. It's in using the Bible that we store God's Word in our heart that we might not sin against Him (Psalm 119). It's where we know truth and can identify and turn away from the lies of the Enemy.

Training in righteousness reminds us of a few things:

Disciples are learners. Followers of Jesus never outgrow or graduate from the Gospel. We are reminded of the power of Jesus' righteousness and how it makes us new every day.

Disciples should crave truth from God. While the world wants to fill our minds daily, we must desire God's Word to transform and renew us. The Bible should disciple us more than the world. What we starve dies, and what we fuel survives.

Disciples are disciplined in training. We will never drift toward sanctification or righteous living. Out of the overflowing desire to spend time with Jesus, develop a plan to engage with His Word every day. When, where, how, and who will check on you to make sure you're not spiritually malnourished?

Be encouraged and reminded that training in righteousness has a purpose. God desires for you to draw near to Him. Training in righteousness has incredible benefits! It's what we "get to do" as followers of Jesus in fulfilling God's call to make disciples.

Disciples continually train in righteousness by growing CLOSER with their Lord and King.

COMMUNICATE | Pray to God

LEARN | Study God's Word

OBEY | Obey God's Truth

STORE | Memorize the Bible

EVANGELIZE | Share the Good News

RENEW | Renew your mind by listening to the voice of God

> **What's your plan for spiritual training? What's one thing you can begin doing today for which you will be eternally grateful?**

> **In your circle of influence, who could be impacted by your training?**

SONG FOR TODAY

"Be Thou My Vision"

Be Thou my wisdom, and Thou my true word
I ever with Thee and Thou with me, Lord
Thou my great Father, and I Thy true son
Thou in me dwelling and I with Thee one

FAITH IN PRACTICE

MEMORIZE

DAY 7

Today, we are going to memorize the powerful Word of God. Just as we read yesterday:

Disciples should crave truth from God. While the world wants to fill our minds daily, we must desire God's Word to transform and renew us. The Bible should disciple us more than the world. What we starve dies, and what we fuel survives.

One of the greatest ways to do that is to place His Word into our hearts and minds by the act of memorization. Take time today to meditate and memorize the Scripture below. When we memorize it, we carry the Gospel with us wherever we go.

2 TIMOTHY 3:16–17
All Scripture is breathed out by God and profitable for teaching,
for reproof, for correction, and for training in righteousness,
that the man of God may be complete, equipped for every good work.

Scan the QR code to experience the fullness of these devotionals by listening to the worship songs complementing them.

II

PRAYER

MATTHEW 6:9-13

Pray then like this:

"Our Father in heaven, hallowed be your name.

Your kingdom come, your will be done,

on earth as it is in heaven.

Give us this day our daily bread,

and forgive us our debts,

as we also have forgiven our debtors.

And lead us not into temptation,

but deliver us from evil.

Prayer is a way for us to communicate to our heavenly Father no matter the season or situation. Prayer brings forth peace in your life while helping you learn more about the plan God has for you. Prayer draws us close to the heart of God while making us more like Jesus. This section will guide you in the discipline of prayer by showing you the true power and importance of prayer.

DAY 8

PRAISE FIRST

Great is the LORD, and greatly to be praised....
PSALM 145:3

Where do your prayers begin? When you're sitting at your kitchen table with your Bible and a cup of coffee, or on your morning commute going bumper-to-bumper, or kneeling at your bedside at the end of the day, what are the first words out of your mouth when you speak to God? "God, help me." "Please bless my day." "I have no words for You right now." "Thank You for answering my last prayer." "Give me what I need."

God loves to hear the petitions of our heart. He delights in our requests – evidence that we believe He is the only One worthy of stepping in to make us whole, to comfort and correct us, to give us peace, to brush away our tears, to understand our frustration. The psalmist David was great at this. "My God, my God, why have you forsaken me?" (Psalm 22:1). "Incline your ear, O LORD, and answer me, for I am poor and needy" (Psalm 86:1). "Create in me a clean heart, O God, and renew a right spirit within me" (Psalm 51:10).

Even the Lord's Prayer spends most of its time teaching us how to ask for what we need. It can be easy to miss the opening statement: "Our Father in heaven, hallowed be your name." The first words out of Christ's mouth when speaking to His Father are words of praise and recognition.

David had a knack for this as well. "I will extol You, O LORD, for you have drawn me up" (Psalm 30:1). "Bless the LORD, O my soul, and all that is within me, bless his holy name!" (Psalm 103:1). "Every day I will bless you and praise your name forever and ever" (Psalm 145:2).

Our God has created a safe space for us to land with our requests, rebukes and rebuttals, but is made joyous by our recognition. It is an issue of positioning as well. The higher we lift the name of the Lord and stand in awe of His greatness, the closer our hearts move to that of Christ's in service and humility. There is no shortage of reasons to praise the One who has given us the very breath with which we speak to Him today.

Rather than asking for something today, spend your prayer time counting your blessings and praising God for what He has already given. It may be the best conversation you've had with Him in a while.

How many blessings and answered prayers can you list in the next five minutes that are worthy of God's praise and recognition? How many things have happened today alone?

SONG FOR TODAY

"HOW GREAT THOU ART"

Oh Lord, my God
When I, in awesome wonder
Consider all the worlds Thy hands have made
I see the stars, I hear the rolling thunder
Thy power throughout the universe displayed

DAY 9

ALL CIRCUMSTANCES

Rejoice always, pray without ceasing, give thanks in all circumstances; for this is the will of God in Christ Jesus for you.

1 THESSALONIANS 5:16-18

When looking through the Old Testament, we read of countless moments in which the Israelites could see God work in such tremendous ways, yet they would still have the audacity to doubt or complain. They lived through the 10 plagues of Egypt, walked through the Red Sea, and had food literally at their feet every morning, but somehow chose to grumble and gripe to God rather than fall prostrate in gratitude.

Studying these moments brings forth the reminder of Matthew 7:3: "Why do you see the speck that is in your brother's eye, but do not notice the log that is in your own eye?"

How many times have we chosen grumbling over gratitude? It is a choice we make every second of every day, and it does take practice. What might have happened had the Israelites chosen to gravitate to the good rather than fester in disappointment? Surely they would have found an "express lane" out of the desert rather than wander around aimlessly for 40 years.

Are you currently in that season of wandering? Challenge yourself to start looking for reasons to thank God. Once you open that floodgate, you'll see just how many blessings God pours out. No matter the situation, God can turn it to good, and that deserves thanks. Some situations may resolve in an afternoon, and some may take generations, but nothing is ever wasted in God's hands.

A weapon has to be forged in fire, pounded, stretched, and plunged into water over and over again before it's ready to be used in battle. Learn to see obstacles as seasons of refining rather than seasons of punishment. If you can just hang in there long enough, eventually you will be polished, balanced and razor sharp, ready to be wielded by our victorious God.

Learn from the mistakes of the Israelites. Train your mind to look back and focus on how He has been good to you in the past. Look to the present and find something you're thankful for now. And look to the future, thanking God for how He is going to use today to shape tomorrow.

> **What struggle are you currently facing? How can you thank God within that circumstance?**

SONG FOR TODAY

"YOU COVER ME"
Prestonwood Worship

Even though I walk
Through the valley of despair
When I can barely offer up a prayer
Still You hear the cry in my heart
Before I speak
You hide me in the shelter
Of Your wings

FAITH IN PRACTICE

THE LORD'S PRAYER

THE LORD'S PRAYER

DAY 10

Today, we'll look at The Lord's Prayer, and we challenge you to do as the Word says – "... go into your room and shut the door and pray to your Father who is in secret" (Matthew 6:6). Take time to find your secret place and worship Him through your prayer. Read this prayer over your life, your family or whatever circumstance comes to mind. Know that the secret to a heart of worship is worshipping in secret. Go and seek Him in your prayers.

THE LORD'S PRAYER | MATTHEW 6:5–15

And when you pray, you must not be like the hypocrites. For they love to stand and pray in the synagogues and at the street corners, that they may be seen by others. Truly, I say to you, they have received their reward. But when you pray, go into your room and shut the door and pray to your Father who is in secret. And your Father who sees in secret will reward you. And when you pray, do not heap up empty phrases as the Gentiles do, for they think that they will be heard for their many words. Do not be like them, for your Father knows what you need before you ask him. Pray then like this:

> Our Father in heaven,
> hallowed be your name.
> Your kingdom come,
> your will be done,
> on earth as it is in heaven.
> Give us this day our daily bread,
> and forgive us our debts,
> as we also have forgiven our debtors.
> And lead us not into temptation,
> but deliver us from evil.

For if you forgive others their trespasses, your heavenly Father will also forgive you, but if you do not forgive others their trespasses, neither will your Father forgive your trespasses.

Scan the QR code to experience the fullness of these devotionals by listening to the worship songs complementing them.

DAY 11

PRAYER OF DELIVERANCE

Because he holds fast to me in love, I will deliver him; I will protect him, because he knows my name. When he calls to me, I will answer him; I will be with him in trouble; I will rescue him and honor him. With long life I will satisfy him and show him my salvation.

PSALM 91:14-16

… call upon me in the day of trouble; I will deliver you, and you shall glorify me.

PSALM 50:15

There is truth within the statement "desperate times call for desperate measures." But there is even greater truth in knowing that *"desperate times call for prayers of desperation,"* and throughout the Bible, we read of this evidence as people cried out in desperation.

We read of the Israelites' calling for help against Goliath, and God answered by sending David. We see Moses' begging God for help as he led the Israelites to the Promised Land, and God answered with food and shelter, and even opened an escape by parting the sea. We read of 10 powerful moments when God answered the prayers of those who begged Him to resurrect either their family member or friend, and He did!

The truth is that when we take time to stop and lift our requests to God, He hears. We can be so quick to try to fix it on our own or work a plan that makes sense, but the greatest help comes from the One who writes the plan and knows our story. We must realize the great power we have in being able to ask help of God, who is and knows all things. The truth of Psalm 50:15 rings true for us: *"… call upon me in the day of trouble; I will deliver you, and you shall glorify me."*

Our prayer is that you will rely on God within the seasons of desperation. Understanding faith in Christ doesn't bring an absence of trials and pain, but faith in Christ brings the ability for us to push through the trials and pain into the provisions He has for us. Remember, desperate times call for prayers of desperation.

Learn from the mistakes of the Israelites. Train your mind to look back and focus on how He has been good to you in the past. Look to the present and find something you're thankful for now. And look to the future, thanking God for how He is going to use today to shape tomorrow.

> **Are you in a season of desperation? What is your initial response, and how can His Word help direct your prayers?**

SONG FOR TODAY

"SAME GOD"

Elevation Worship

DAY 12

WORSHIP IS MY WEAPON

For we do not wrestle against flesh and blood, but against the rulers, against the authorities, against the cosmic powers over this present darkness, against the spiritual forces of evil in the heavenly places.

EPHESIANS 6:12

We are in a war. If we are not awake to that fact, we will lose precious ground. The Enemy of our souls and all his demonic forces are coming for us … for our spouses, our kids, our peace, our relationships, our testimony, and our ability to live in the light. The Enemy comes to "steal, kill and destroy." What weapons will we bring to this fight? How will we preserve the land of our integrity, our souls, our families, our purpose? We can win this, right?

Yes.

One of *the* keys to victory is prayer. Deep, sustaining, communication with God. He is our victory. He is the destination. To be one with Him in prayer is living out Psalm 23:4-5.

Even though I walk through the valley of the shadow of death, I will fear no evil, for you are with me; your rod and your staff, they comfort me. You prepare a table before me in the presence of my enemies…."

His presence, His Word, His way is *all*.

The world faced a global conflict from 1939 through 1945, World War II. Nazi Party leader Adolf Hitler's evil rise and reign caused an unprecedented world conflict - killing millions and scarring generations. Prime Minister Winston Churchill rallied the United Kingdom from the brink of defeat to victory. You can still see the famous war rooms where he met with his cabinet, strategized and masterminded the steps that led to victory. The war rooms were secret. They were underground. They housed books and strategic maps, battle plans and communication strategies. They were where the war was won.

The way of prayer, in some ways, is the way of the war rooms. In the secret place, the Spirit of God is calling us to convene with Him. It is there we hear His voice, study the map of His Word, and link arms with other believers. We worship Him and call for His kingdom to come "on earth as it is in heaven." It is where we become a non-anxious presence. It is where we find peace and share a meal at the table when the bombs of hell are exploding around us. The secret place is a place of communion. It's a place of humility. It's a place of victory through a different path. A path of surrender.

"A prayer room is first and foremost a living room – a place where the Father waits for his children to come and climb into his arms." — Pete Greig

How often do you go to prayer to fight the wars in your life? What wars are you facing that you need to bring before God in prayer?

SONG FOR TODAY

"BATTLE BELONGS"
Phil Wickham

DAY 13

GLAD ASSURANCE IN CHRIST

The LORD spoke to Moses, saying, "Speak to Aaron and his sons, saying, Thus you shall bless the people of Israel: you shall say to them,

The LORD bless you and keep you;
the LORD make his face to shine upon you and be gracious to you;
the LORD lift up his countenance upon you and give you peace.

So shall they put my name upon the people of Israel, and I will bless them."

NUMBERS 6:22-27

The Israelites were no strangers to God's blessing. Beginning in the Garden of Eden, even God's commands to Adam and Eve were a blessing (Genesis 1:28). All of God's commands are blessings, because they define the parameters by which one must live in order to know and enjoy God, rightly.

The Aaronic Blessing in Numbers 6 is the greatest pep-talk ever given! God will soon lead the Israelites through the wilderness, but they don't know what God knows – this is going to be a long, difficult journey, filled with trial, failure, death and unbelief. The Lord had made a covenant with Israel, and He knew full well that they would be unable to keep it. However, the Lord blesses, is gracious, and gives peace (Numbers 6:24–26), and He does this out of His love for us, and for the glory of His own name. When His people fall short, He keeps His covenant. In this way, Numbers 6 both foreshadows the difficulty to come, and comforts with the assurance that God will act on Israel's behalf.

King David employs this famous prayer in Psalm 67, adding "that your way may be known on earth, your saving power among all nations ... let all the peoples praise you!" The culmination of God's blessings toward His people has always been that all the world would know His glory! Though Aaron and David proved to be poor mediators between God and His people, Jesus is the true-and-better mediator, who earned our salvation by His blood, so that "all the peoples" would truly praise Him!

As we pray, casting our gaze toward the Cross of Christ this Easter, we can pray in full assurance that God keeps His Word, not because of anything we've done, but because of what He's done. Like the Israelites in the desert, we don't know the dangers ahead of us, but God purchased us with the blood of the Son, and we can rest, knowing that He will keep us until the end. Let us thank God, that He is so wonderful that all the world will one day see His glory!

> **Do you ever doubt God's purpose to bless you? What assurance do you have that He will keep His Word?**

SONG FOR TODAY

"DOXOLOGY"

Praise God from whom all blessings flow
Praise Him, all creatures here below
Praise Him above, ye heavenly host
Praise Father, Son, and Holy Ghost

FAITH IN PRACTICE

POSTURE OF PRAYER

POSTURE OF PRAYER

DAY 14

Throughout this section, we have learned how and when to pray. We've touched on the power and importance of praying and how prayer can draw us nearer to the heart of God. Today we challenge you to posture your heart and body in prayer, and for some, that's a new thing to do. The posture of your body is a way you can express the posture of your heart, so what is your current posture of prayer? Do you need to open your hands to receive healing? Do you need to lift your hands in surrender or kneel down in reverence?

Push yourself into the unfamiliar and new. Stretch yourself to posture your heart and body in prayer. It is when we push ourselves in practicing spiritual disciplines that we see growth in our relationship with Jesus as we become more like Him.

Take time today to find your posture of prayer. The new and unfamiliar can bring forth a fresh wind. Go and pray.

PSALM 95:6
Oh come, let us worship and bow down;
let us kneel before the LORD, our Maker!

PSALM 63:4
So I will bless you as long as I live....

Scan the QR code to experience the fullness of these devotionals by listening to the worship songs complementing them.

III

CONFESSION & REPENTANCE

JAMES 5:16

Therefore, confess your sins to one another and pray for one another, that you may be healed. The prayer of a righteous person has great power as it is working.

Confession and repentance are fundamental parts of the Christian life. They are acts of humility that keep us in a healthy fellowship with God and one another. This week will challenge you to develop and grow in appreciation of confession and repentance.

DAY 15

HUMILITY IN CONFESSION

... if you confess with your mouth that Jesus is Lord and believe in your heart that God raised him from the dead, you will be saved. For with the heart one believes and is justified, and with the mouth one confesses and is saved.

ROMANS 10:9-10

So much of the Christian life is rooted in humility. Your entrance into the Christian family, as presented in Romans 10:9–10, begins with a confession that you don't have everything together and that you need Christ to rescue you.

Afterward, you continue to confess your sins, seeking repentance to grow closer to Jesus and humbly acknowledging that you still don't have it all together and He is your only hope.

Confession of Christ as Lord	Confessing and Repenting of Sin
I am a sinner in need of salvation.	I am a member of God's family.
I cannot save myself.	I still sin, but I want to be more like Jesus.
Jesus is the Son of God who gave His life to pay the penalty for my sin and provide salvation to those who place their faith in Him.	Unconfessed sin is a hindrance to being like Jesus. God wants to forgive my sins and restore a vibrant fellowship with me.
Action: I call upon Jesus to forgive me, save me, and be the Lord of my life.	Action: I confess, gain forgiveness, and continue to become more like Jesus.

Humility is an acknowledgment of reality. Just as a pair of prescription glasses corrects your sight, an attitude of humility allows you to see things as they are – chiefly, the chasm between God's holiness and my sinfulness.

God has aided us in understanding our reality through some tools. The Law was a series of external requirements intended to help those following it realize that they needed a Savior. No one could follow all the Law with perfection. If someone was mistakenly attempting to obtain righteousness through the Law, failure to live out the Law in perfection in any area meant that he was guilty of all (James 2:10). What a generous wake-up call!

Not only does the Law help correct any notion that we're enough on our own, but the Holy Spirit also does that job. Jesus said that the Holy Spirit works in the lives of unbelievers, exposing their sin to them and convincing them of their sinfulness (John 16:8). In the life of the believer, one of the works of the Holy Spirit is to prod you toward greater Christ-likeness and empower you to move in that direction (Galatians 5:16–18).

Today, you are in a classic "Good news, bad news" situation. The bad news: you don't have it all together, and you never will, this side of heaven. The good news: God has done and desires to continue to do wonders in your life. The Holy Spirit wants to mature you in Christ Jesus, but He will not force growth upon you; you must choose humility and, in doing so, release the floodgates of work of the Spirit in your life.

> **Create a list of areas in your life where you would like to see growth (e.g., my role as a father, husband or employee). Ask God for humility to recognize your shortcomings and confess your need for His intervention.**

SONG FOR TODAY

"TURN YOUR EYES UPON JESUS"

Turn your eyes upon Jesus
Look full in his wonderful face
And the things of earth will grow strangely dim
In the light of his glory and grace

DAY 16

THROUGH-AND-THROUGH

Now may the God of peace himself sanctify you completely, and may your whole spirit and soul and body be kept blameless at the coming of our Lord Jesus Christ. He who calls you is faithful; he will surely do it.

1 THESSALONIANS 5:23-24

In this country, we collectively begin to look forward to college football season the day after the last bowl game in January. Die-hard alumni might say that they are fans of their school team through-and-through to affirm the deep level of affection and identity they associate with their college. Of course, this didn't happen overnight. It is a journey. Some of your connections with your college might be passed down to you by family members who graduated from the institution. Your fervor for your team might have been strengthened by four years of education and indoctrination while a student. A large part of what shapes your collegiate identity and passion is contingent on your complete rejection of those who compete against or *oppose* your school.

For believers in Christ, sanctification is a strikingly similar process. When a person places faith in Christ, this process of sanctification is initiated and, according to Paul in 1 Thessalonians 5:23, it is accomplished by God Himself. This is good news, because Scripture affirms that we "all have sinned and fall short of the glory of God" (Romans 3:23) and our "righteous deeds are like a polluted garment" (Isaiah 64:6). But, when God initiates this process, 1 Peter 1:2 details that we, through the sanctifying work of the Spirit, can be obedient to God. This is basically what sanctification entails – a daily surrender and obedience to the indwelling Spirit of God, over and over, until we start to look like Christ, through-and-through.

There's one more part to sanctification, though. Just as we have opponents in football, we also have things which oppose sanctification. In our pursuit of holiness, through sanctification, our flesh (or sin nature) is a very formidable enemy. Colossians 3:5 warns us to "put to death therefore what is earthly in you." As we approach our Easter celebration, no matter where we are in our life-long journey to be sanctified in Christ, we must identify our Enemy. Name those sins that have a hold on us. Confess the areas in which we struggle and ask God, through the sanctifying work of the Spirit, to cleanse us through-and-through.

What sins are standing in opposition to your sanctification? Identify and confess them to Christ. Ask for the Holy Spirit's help in conquering sin in your life.

SONG FOR TODAY

"AMAZING GRACE"

'Twas grace that taught my heart to fear
And grace my fears relieved
How precious did that grace appear
The hour I first believed

FAITH IN PRACTICE

IN + DOWN

IN + DOWN

DAY 17

Yesterday's devotion challenged you to identify and confess sin that is holding you back from growing in Christ-likeness; some things probably came to mind immediately. Today, spend time in prayer, asking the Lord to search your heart and identify areas of sin to which you have become blind. Meditate on the Psalm below and take time to look in and down within heart and soul.

PSALM 139:23–24

Search me, O God, and know my heart!
    Try me and know my thoughts!
And see if there be any grievous way in me,
    and lead me in the way everlasting!

Scan the QR code to experience the fullness of these devotionals by listening to the worship songs complementing them.

DAY 18

COMING CLEAN

Therefore, confess your sins to one another and pray for one another, that you may be healed. The prayer of a righteous person has great power as it is working.

JAMES 5:16

When electricity came to rural areas in the early- to mid-20th century, most people were astounded at this "miracle of light." When the sun went down and activities of the day concluded, electricity and light (much brighter than coal-oil lamps and lanterns) spread through the country. Dark places were illuminated, and people enjoyed a new way of life. Through the power of electricity, a world of possibilities opened! When a believer confesses his sins to a trusted brother, darkness is dispelled, and he enjoys a new way of living.

Confession and repentance as a spiritual discipline might feel punitive, *judge-y* or even legalistic. But God knows we need a clean slate. We need a reset. The fact that He offers new mercies to us each morning tells us all we need to know about our cycle of confession and repentance. It must remain frequent, and up to date.

Confessing our sin to God and others is biblically sound, but another principle of confession is at work in James' admonition in 5:16. Sin grows and gains power over us in the dark. We need to surround ourselves with people to whom we pledge accountability. This is wisdom. Confession of our sins to other believers through transparency and accountability moves us away from the brokenness of our sin and toward healing. The power and struggle of our sin is brought into the light where we have the prayers and accountability of others.

Beyond our need to confess sin to God and others, sometimes there is another step of confession. Though all sin is against God, some sins are perpetrated against others, and private, prayerful confession to God needs to be followed by sincere confession, specifically to those against whom we have sinned. Further, we should repent and seek forgiveness.

Burdens and strongholds will lift when you exercise obedience in confession. It might seem like a frightening proposition. However, remember that a better way of life is waiting for you. Be bold and step into the light.

> **Thank God for brothers and sisters in Christ who can walk alongside us. Whom has God placed in your life to serve as those to whom you can confess sin?**

SONG FOR TODAY

"HEART OF WORSHIP"
Matt Redman

DAY 19

THE PATH TO PROSPER

*Whoever conceals his transgressions will not prosper,
but he who confesses and forsakes them will obtain mercy.*

PROVERBS 28:13

Since the time of Adam and Eve, our response to sin has been to hide it. We were created to be in constant fellowship with God. That is the entire truth provided to us in the creation account in Genesis 1–3. When we break that fellowship through our sin, we feel ashamed because we know that we have damaged a sacred relationship with our Creator. This fractured relationship is the crack that the Enemy steps into to create a larger chasm.

In this moment of unrepented sin, the Enemy begins to propagate lies about our value and worth. The Enemy begins to increase the level of shame we feel, in some cases driving us to hurt ourselves in order to feel something else. The Enemy begins to inflate the cost of reconciliation to a point where it almost seems impossible to forgive. Yet, today's proverb clearly reminds us just how simple it is to find healing and mercy.

The proverb begins "Whoever conceals...." The truth is, both God and man conceal transgressions. We conceal our transgressions because of the shame we feel. God also conceals our transgressions with His grace.

The proverb then reminds us that should we choose to continue to conceal our sin, we will live a life that does not prosper. Yet, what does it mean to prosper? Well, the writer gives us that as well in the following line when he writes "...but he who confesses and forsakes them will obtain mercy."

To live a life that prospers is to live a life secured in the mercy granted to us through the life, death, and Resurrection of His Son, Jesus.

The pathway to a life that prospers is to "confess and forsake."

Confess that you acknowledge your sin and offense to the Father and forsake your sinful desires daily as to not repeat that offense.

The pathway to mercy is simple, yet the burden of shame can be so deceptive. Choose today to not let the shame steal His gift of mercy.

What sin in your life has been keeping you from the prosperous life promised in today's verse?

SONG FOR TODAY

"NOTHING BUT THE BLOOD"

What can wash away my sin?
Nothing but the blood of Jesus;
What can make me whole again?
Nothing but the blood of Jesus.

DAY 20

LET ME TELL YOU ABOUT MY JESUS

There is therefore now no condemnation for those who are in Christ Jesus. For the law of the Spirit of life has set you free in Christ Jesus from the law of sin and death.

ROMANS 8:1-2

I sought the LORD, and he answered me and delivered me from all my fears. Those who look to him are radiant, and their faces shall never be ashamed. This poor man cried, and the LORD heard him and saved him out of all his troubles.

PSALM 34:4-6

Shame is one of the Enemy's greatest tactics to make us feel as if confession and repentance are not part of the healing process. The Enemy tells us to "keep it to ourselves because no one will understand." Or "if people really knew your thoughts, they would cast you aside." But here is the good news – our God is not One to condemn. When we come to Him and lay down our sins before Him, He meets us right where we are with love and compassion. It is through confession that we can be set free by the power of the Holy Spirit (Romans 8:1–2).

It is safe to say that a lot of times our first response is to keep something we are ashamed of to ourselves. But what if we came before the Lord and sought Him wholeheartedly through prayer? We are reminded of the power of confession through David in his psalm and his longing to seek the Lord's guidance (Psalm 34:4–6).

When we come before the Lord, we are welcomed rather than dismissed. It is through confession that we start to see a transformation in our own hearts and minds. By the power of the Holy Spirit, our appearance becomes radiant as we fully trust in the Lord, rather than an appearance of weariness if we decide to settle in the cloud of shame.

Let me tell you about my Jesus. He is the One who hears our cries. He is the One who will be with us on those awful, lonely nights. He is the One who desires to have a relationship with us. He is the One who created us for a purpose. There is no condemnation for those who are children of God. Look to Him. Seek Him. Come before Him, confessing to the Lord whatever has been weighing you down. And when you do this, there will be a peace that far outweighs anything this world can give you.

What can I confess to the Lord today that has been weighing me down, so that I can begin the healing process of casting away my shame?

SONG FOR TODAY

"MY JESUS"

Jeff Pargo, Anne Wilson & Matthew West

FAITH IN PRACTICE

IRON SHARPENS IRON

IRON SHARPENS IRON

DAY 21

You were built for relationships. The Scriptures encourage you to invite other believers into your life and enjoy growth together. This experience can sometimes be painful and requires honesty rooted in trust. The process is illustrated in Proverbs 27:17, with people's sharpening and helping to shape one another compared to sharpening pieces of iron. The iron becomes sharp (useful) when it's worked by another piece of iron; both pieces are better for the process.

Who in your life is helping to mold you to become more like Christ? How often do you meet? Do you confess sin to one another and hold each other accountable (James 5:16)? Are you intentionally encouraging that person and being encouraged by him or her (Hebrews 3:13)?

Pray for boldness to be vulnerable with another trusted believer. Pray that God would either establish or strengthen a current relationship so that you might shape and sharpen one another in the image of Christ.

PROVERBS 27:17
Iron sharpens iron, and one man sharpens another.

Scan the QR code to experience the fullness of these devotionals by listening to the worship songs complementing them.

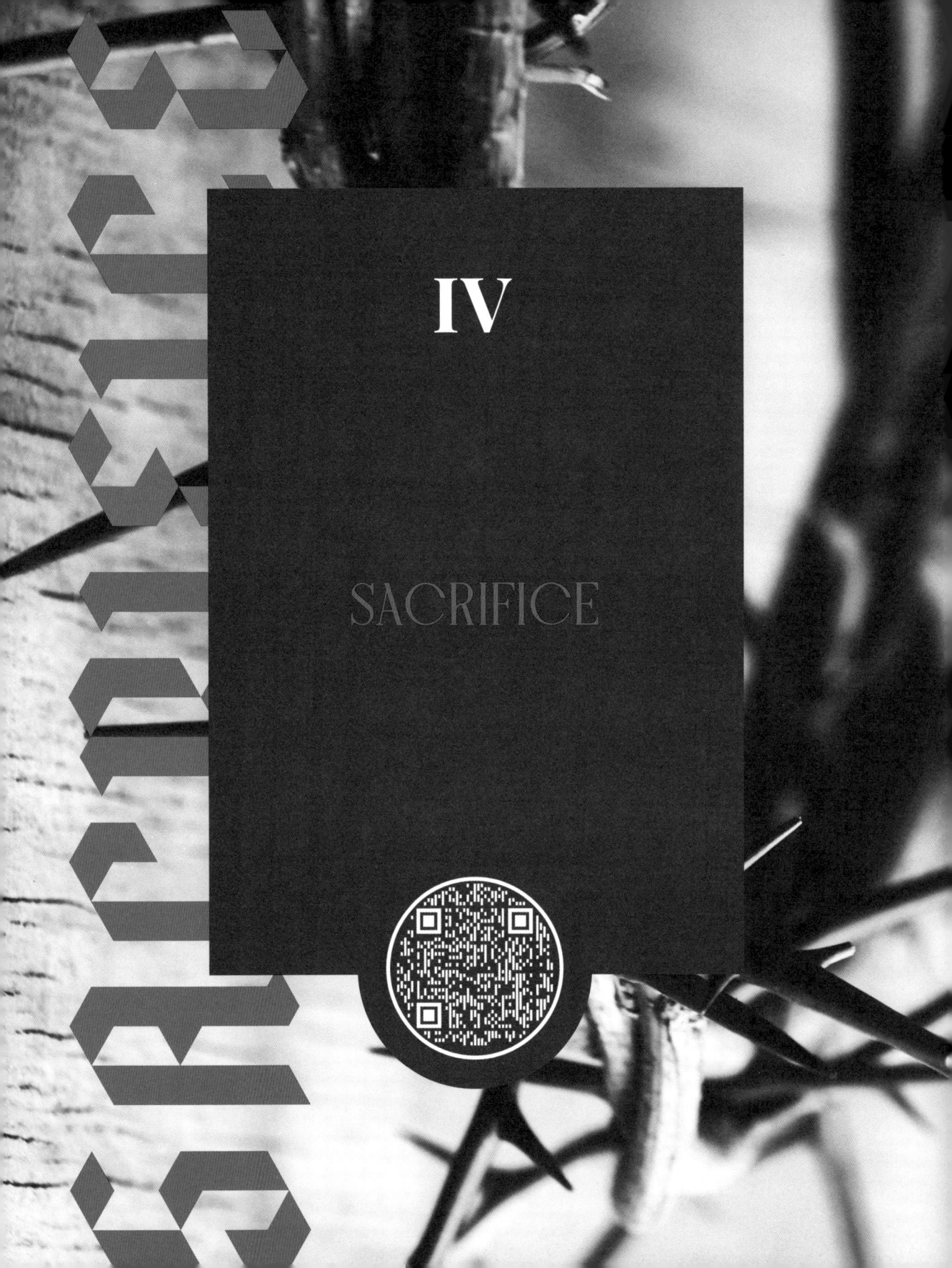

PHILIPPIANS 2:17–18

Even if I am to be poured out as a drink offering upon the sacrificial offering of your faith, I am glad and rejoice with you all. Likewise you also should be glad and rejoice with me.

For our next week of devotionals, we will reflect on the Lord's sacrifice on our behalf. Sacrifice is an essential theme of Easter. We typically think of sacrifice as an act of slaughtering an animal or surrendering a possession as an offering to God to appease Him. However, as we read in Philippians 2:17–18, sacrifice is more widely seen as giving to the Lord whatever He requires of our time, our earthly possessions, and our energies to further His work. Consider what He would have you sacrifice for the purpose of fully focusing on Him.

DAY 22

THE SACRIFICE OF CHRIST

Let each of you look not only to his own interests, but also to the interests of others. Have this mind among yourselves, which is yours in Christ Jesus, who, though he was in the form of God, did not count equality with God a thing to be grasped, but emptied himself, by taking the form of a servant, being born in the likeness of men. And being found in human form, he humbled himself by becoming obedient to the point of death, even death on a cross.

PHILIPPIANS 2:4-8

When Epaphroditus brought a generous gift from the church in Philippi, and good news of the church's concern for Paul, he also brought troubling news of a possible division in the church. False teachers were coming in from the outside and causing disagreements and conflict within the church. Paul knew that true spiritual unity is a matter of a sacrificial heart, not convincing others that your preferred way of doing things is the right way.

Since the believers at Philippi were unified by their relationship with Jesus, this unity should have encouraged them to sacrifice their own personal rights to solve any differences they might have had in a gracious, God-honoring manner. Their disagreements revealed a spiritual problem that wasn't going to be solved by a certain methodology, but by their hearts' coming together in a right relationship with Jesus Christ as they focused on serving each other. Our great spiritual need is to be like Christ, and we do so by following in His example, laying down our rights for the good of others and the will of the Father.

Jesus, who was, in His very nature, God, laid down His rights as God, refusing to use those God-given rights for His own personal good, as He chose to humble Himself by taking on the very nature of a servant and becoming obedient to death on the Cross. Jesus laid down His God-given rights in order to pick up our adopted rights to become children of God through His death, burial and Resurrection!

As we pray for a spirit of sacrificial giving, Paul tells us that our sacrifice will always strive to highly exalt Jesus and give Him "… the name that is above every name, so that at the name of Jesus every knee should bow, in heaven and on earth and under the earth, and every tongue confess that Jesus Christ is Lord, to the glory of God the Father" (Philippians 2:9–11).

What are some ways you can sacrifice your personal preferences for the good of others in your life such as a family member, coworker, classmate or neighbor who is in need?

SONG FOR TODAY

"MORE LIKE JESUS"
Passion

DAY 23

SACRIFICING YOURSELF

Even if I am to be poured out as a drink offering upon the sacrificial offering of your faith, I am glad and rejoice with you all. Likewise you also should be glad and rejoice with me.

PHILIPPIANS 2:17-18

There is something about stories of sacrifice that touch us in ways other stories are unable to. The tales of people who offer up their lives – or put themselves in great danger in order to save loved ones and strangers alike – make us feel viscerally connected to what we believe represents the best in humanity. That's because it does. As you read yesterday, Christ showed us the perfect example of sacrifice.

Paul, who wrote the book of Philippians from the inside of a prison cell, was a devout Jew before he began following Jesus, and was an expert on Jewish tradition. In these verses, he alludes to the common Jewish practice of topping off the burnt sacrifice of an animal with a drink offering, usually of wine, that, when poured on the fire, would create a steam and a fragrance that would rise up to the Lord (Leviticus 23). Paul also understood the powerful connection between Jesus' sacrifice on the Cross with the ritual sacrifices of the Jewish people. He knew that as imperfect as we are, the call of the Christian is the call to become more Christ-like. The call to become more Christ-like is the call to present our bodies as living sacrifices unto the Lord (Romans 12:1).

Here, scholars believe Paul may be using the Old Testament imagery of a drink offering to allude to his impending death; that in his martyrdom for Christ, he might become like a "drink offering" that would be poured out on the service and sacrifice of those faithful members of the early church.

And, even though the sacrifice would mean his death, Paul was resolute in rejoicing. He considered it pure joy (James 1:2) to be the drink offering that would catalyze and mobilize the early church. He rejoiced in the church's service and sacrifice, and he told them they should also rejoice in his. Why? Because he understood he had the opportunity to mirror the perfect sacrifice accomplished on the Cross, being allowed to be used by God to bring glory to the Lamb, the perfect son of God, despite his own shortcomings and imperfection.

> **What is holding you back from giving your whole life to Christ so that you can be a "living sacrifice"?**

SONG FOR TODAY

"SON OF SUFFERING"
Bethel Music

FAITH IN PRACTICE

SELF-SACRIFICE

SELF-SACRIFICE

DAY 24

During the past two days, you have read how Christ and Paul both gave of themselves, even to the point of death. They did so because they prioritized the will of God and needs of others above their own. Read and reflect on Acts 20:35:

ACTS 20:35
In all things I have shown you that by working hard in this way we must help the weak and remember the words of the Lord Jesus, how he himself said, "It is more blessed to give than to receive."

Challenge yourself today to give away a resource (your time, talent, or treasure) to someone.

Scan the QR code to experience the fullness of these devotionals by listening to the worship songs complementing them.

DAY 25

SACRIFICE TAKES PRACTICE

Do you not know that in a race all the runners run, but only one receives the prize? So run that you may obtain it. Every athlete exercises self-control in all things. They do it to receive a perishable wreath, but we an imperishable. So I do not run aimlessly; I do not box as one beating the air. But I discipline my body and keep it under control, lest after preaching to others I myself should be disqualified.

1 CORINTHIANS 9:24-27

Practice is "performing a particular activity, method, or custom habitually and regularly in order to become proficient" (*Merriam-Webster*). The goal of practice is to become so familiar with an activity that it "becomes second nature" – it becomes part of who you are. Being a Christ-follower, like being an athlete, asks that we enact behaviors that we have practiced. The idea that once we choose to follow Christ, we can relax our way into our destiny is a lie. As we read, there is a need to constantly practice self-control, purposeful living and the self-discipline to deny our earthly desires in pursuit of heavenly goals.

Implied in this idea is the necessity to choose truth and remain "...steadfast, immovable, always abounding in the work of the Lord, knowing that in the Lord your labor is not in vain" (1 Corinthians 15:58). In the physical realm, if you desire a body that is healthy, sacrifices must be made to support that goal. For example, healthy foods, good sleep patterns and the removal of harmful substances. The same is true in the realm of the eternal – if you desire peace, wholeness, and joy – you will need to sacrifice desires that are contrary to that goal. You'll need to exchange resentment for peace, doublemindedness for wholeness, and bitterness for joy.

Christ had all things under His authority. As it says in Colossians, "all things were made through Him and for Him." At any time, He could have stopped His passion to the Cross – and yet Jesus chose to sacrifice Himself (sacrifice His personal preferences) to remain committed to His father's will (Luke 42:22).

Christ's Crucifixion was the ultimate act of submission and sacrifice. Christ practiced His submission through the whole of His earthly ministry, shown by His continued prayer and obedience. Because He did so, we can look to Christ as the example and begin practicing spiritual discipline in our life.

Are you doing things that are contrary to your identity as a son or daughter of the Father? What are they?

SONG FOR TODAY

"YOUR LOVE IS OUR FAVORITE SONG"
Prestonwood Worship

Lord we come, to worship at Your throne
We bow down to You and You alone
For who You are and all You've done
Your blessings are more than enough

DAY 26

A SERVANT'S SACRIFICE

For though I am free from all, I have made myself a servant to all, that I might win more of them.

1 CORINTHIANS 9:19

Paul inspires believers with the statement, as he gives his argument as to why we should sacrifice. Christians should grow to the point in their life where they are willing to take up their cross daily because they want to emulate the character and work of Jesus. Paul echoes this same concept in our passage, as he talks about the sacrifices that he has made throughout his ministry. Paul denied the right to take any provisions from the churches that he was planting and preaching so that nobody would question his motive.

In that time, it was expected for the congregation to give, just as we do today, in order to help sustain a minister's ability to focus on the spiritual development and care of the community. Planting churches while working full time is not exactly an easy road, but Paul desired to display his commitment in every area of life, including how he spent his free time. He was willing to give anything up for the sake of the Gospel. Paul allowed his potential to proclaim override his preferences.

God did a mighty work in Paul, as he became a man who voluntarily became a slave to others, bending his desires to suit the needs of others. This mimics the same kind of humility that we see in Philippians 2 from Jesus. The humility and sacrifice of any believer becomes a firm building block for the Church. In this passage, Paul has submitted his body as a service to Jesus, and Jesus has told him to use it for His glory. We can see this wonderful shift in desire in Paul, as sacrifice transitions from burden to blessing, and God wishes to do this same work in each and every Christian that has come to faith in Him.

If you are wondering what produced this virtue in Paul, we see that his life radically changed when he met Jesus. Paul continued to dive in, discovering more about Jesus and becoming one of the most influential Christians to ever live. All because of what Jesus did for him. Jesus proved Himself to be of far more value than anything in Paul's life; and Paul changed his priorities to suit this change. Jesus is worth whatever cost we can imagine.

> **What is one aspect of your life (career, goals, comfort, entertainment, etc.) to which you give a lot of time?**

SONG FOR TODAY

"YOUR WILL, YOUR WAY"

Bryan & Katie Torwalt

DAY 27

FOCUSING THROUGH FASTING

"And when you fast, do not look gloomy like the hypocrites, for they disfigure their faces that their fasting may be seen by others. Truly, I say to you, they have received their reward. But when you fast, anoint your head and wash your face, that your fasting may not be seen by others but by your Father who is in secret. And your Father who sees in secret will reward you."

MATTHEW 6:16-18

The spiritual discipline of fasting has been around for centuries. Moses experienced the first fast recorded in Scripture in Exodus 34 as he was on Mount Sinai with the Lord for 40 days and 40 nights without any food or water. The well-known Greek physician Hippocrates recommended abstinence from food or drink for physical reasons as early as the 5th-century BC. Fasting is practiced among many religions, whether for hours or weeks. Fasting has been around for centuries and will continue to be a regular practice for many cultures in the future. Although they differ in duration, practice and reasons, most have similar goals of showing sacrifice and cleansing oneself.

Christians are instructed in the book of Matthew to let our fasting be in secret, solely focusing our all on God as we long to experience Him in a more intimate way. Just as we are instructed to enter our closet when we pray, the same goes for fasting. It is to be a private connection between our heart and the heart of God, in private and with proper motives. If it is for the purpose of trying to impress others, it will not be effective nor blessed by God. But as promised in Matthew 6:18, when done with a spirit of humility, sincerely seeking God with a longing for more, He sees and rewards.

Fasting is the act of denying oneself and one's needs to grow our dependence and reliance on

God. It is a part of our sacrificial living for the purpose of bringing our spirits in alignment with His. It is a reminder to us that He provides for each and every one of our needs.

> **In what ways are you or are you not depending on God? How is God calling you to depend on Him?**

SONG FOR TODAY

"YEARN"

Shane & Shane

ISAIAH 53:3-5

He was despised and rejected by men,

a man of sorrows and acquainted with grief;

and as one from whom men hide their faces

he was despised, and we esteemed him not.

Surely he has borne our griefs

and carried our sorrows;

yet we esteemed him stricken,

smitten by God, and afflicted.

But he was pierced for our transgressions;

he was crushed for our iniquities;

upon him was the chastisement that brought us peace,

and with his wounds we are healed.

Holy Week, the final section of our journey together, tells the story of the powerful display of sacrifice, grace and mercy Jesus had. Within this section, we will read the story of Jesus and the way He sacrificed Himself for the sake of the Gospel. During these next eight days, we hope you take intentional time to thank God for this story, and we hope you are reminded of the true depth of His love displayed on the Cross, a cross that should have been carried by us. May we never forget the power He showed us during this Holy Week.

DAY 28

PALM SUNDAY

MATTHEW 21:1-11, 14-17; MARK 11:1-11; LUKE 19:29-44; JOHN 12:12-36

One of the blessings of Scripture is that it allows a unique opportunity to look back and be reminded that God's promises remain intact, from generation to generation.

In history we see that Passover was approaching, and the people of Israel were restless. It was a time of discontent in the Holy Land where people were anxious for change. The Promised Land was occupied by foreign oppressors, and the Jewish people were forced to live under the hand of the Romans.

According to Scripture, deliverance would take the form of a man, a Messiah, one who would provide peace and restore joy amidst brokenness. There are hundreds of prophecies describing the coming Messiah; one such prophecy describes Him as a mighty king who will make Himself known by entering Jerusalem in humility on a donkey. This is what the people knew to look for, and today, Palm Sunday, this is exactly what they will find.

It's nearly Passover, and Jesus and the disciples join countless other pilgrims who flock to Jerusalem to celebrate the festival. It is an event to remember God's intervention and rescue of Israel from the clutches of Egypt. Jesus will choose this day to make Himself known as the Messiah – today He will fulfill prophecy.

In preparation for His journey, Jesus sends two of His disciples to find the donkey that He will ride into Jerusalem, and He begins his journey. As He travels, the disciples spontaneously take off their outer cloaks and lay them out in His path on the dusty road as a tribute to the Messiah. Other pilgrims on the road to Jerusalem follow suit, cutting palm branches from nearby fields and placing them on the ground in front of the colt. As they do so, they shout out these words: "Hosanna! Blessed is he who comes in the name of the Lord! Blessed is the coming kingdom of our father David! Hosanna in the highest!"

The beauty of this moment is that Jesus wouldn't be saving them from momentary affliction, but from a profound and eternal rift between God and humanity. Jesus' deliverance will completely eclipse the work celebrated at the Passover feast.

As we step into the weight and beauty of Holy Week, we invite you to remember the choice that was made on your behalf. The choice of a Cross over comfort. The choice of sacrifice over safety. Jesus knew where the road He took that day would lead, and yet He did it anyway.

Celebrate Jesus today. Praise God for a king who is mighty to save. Praise God for His faithfulness when we least deserve it. Praise God that He made a way when there was no way.

> **When was the last time you reflected on the faithfulness Jesus has displayed for you? How can you use His faithfulness to inspire your faith?**

SONG FOR TODAY

"HOSANNA"

Hillsong Worship

DAY 29

MONDAY

MATTHEW 21:12-13, 18-19; MARK 11:12-18; LUKE 19:45-48

We see righteous anger erupting out of Jesus in today's reading. All eyes are on Him after the prophetic display of riding into Jerusalem and symbolically announcing Himself Israel's king. In Roman-occupied Israel, declaring yourself a king is a good way to get yourself killed.

Nevertheless, Jesus stages a confrontation with Israel's leaders right in the temple, the heart of Jewish life and culture. The priests have set up a lucrative moneymaking scheme, charging exorbitant interest on out-of-towners, exchanging their local currency for temple currency, and simultaneously price gouging the cost of animals being purchased for Passover sacrifices. That Jesus upends the tables where they are selling doves is no accident. Doves are the sacrifice of those too poor to purchase lambs.

This is not what the God of Israel intended for the temple. The temple was supposed to be a place where Yahweh's presence dwelt, and His chosen people reflected His goodness and grace to the world.

From Capernaum to Jerusalem, Jesus has grown in popularity, but He has also tried to keep a low profile. Today, however, he does something out of character – flipping tables over in the middle of the temple.

Israel's leaders know exactly what He is doing. He is calling them out. Jewish leadership is still corrupt. The poor are still being abused. Things are not OK between God and His people, and it's time for a change.

Jesus' kingdom – the real kingdom – has arrived. In this kingdom, people love one another. They serve one another. The greatest among them take the position of the lowly. Israel has it totally backward. Israel has turned their God's "house of prayer" into a "den of robbers." Jesus' passion is incendiary. He'll tear the place apart before He'll let the poor and the wounded be abused.

On His way back to the temple, Jesus comes across a fig tree with leaves but no fruit, so He curses it. He seizes upon a moment to ingrain the gravity of the situation on His disciples by bringing to life an image they had undoubtedly read about in their Jewish youth and life: the fruitless tree.

Israel has produced no fruit. In their hardness of heart, they have rejected His offer of the true kingdom. This rejection will cost Jesus His life, and He willingly gives it out of love to save them ... and to save us.

Absorb the depth of Jesus' passion for you today. It may sometimes be confrontational, but it is always rooted in an all-consuming love for His children.

> **How do you believe the passion of Jesus affects you? Can you relate to the passion He displays in the Scripture noted in this devotional?**

SONG FOR TODAY

"I STAND AMAZED IN THE PRESENCE"

O how marvelous! O how wonderful!
And my song shall ever be:
O how marvelous! O how wonderful!
Is my Savior's love for me!

DAY 30

TUESDAY

MATTHEW 21:20-25:46; MARK 11:20-13:37; LUKE 20:1-21:36

After Jesus' triumphal entry into Jerusalem on Palm Sunday, He went to work on Monday, turning everything upside down – literally – as He challenged the hypocrisy and hollowness of the religious establishment.

On Tuesday morning, Jesus returned to the city. He was hungry as He walked toward Jerusalem; and seeing a lone fig tree, He found nothing on it except its leaves, and He said to it, "No longer shall there ever be any fruit from you." At once the fig tree withered. His disciples were bewildered. Jesus told them: "Truly, I say to you, if you have faith, and do not doubt, you shall not only do what was done to the fig tree, but even if you say to this mountain, 'Be taken up and cast into the sea,' it will happen. And all things you ask in prayer, believing, you will receive."

On the heels of this, Jesus arrived at the temple, and the chief priests and elders quickly came up to Him and said, "By what authority are you doing these things, and who gave you this authority?" Their questions were part of a plan to discredit Jesus and catch Him saying something that would lead to His arrest.

But they could not outwit Jesus. Jesus said He would answer their question, but only if they would first answer His question. He asked, "Was the baptism of John the Baptist from heaven or from man?" The religious leaders were baffled. They could not answer "from heaven," because John testified to Jesus as the Lamb of God. On the other hand, they could not answer that the baptism of John the Baptist was "from man," because Mathew's Gospel told us that these leaders feared the crowds. Stumped, all they could answer was, "We do not know." And so, Jesus said to them, "Neither will I tell you by what authority I do these things."

Then Jesus shared several parables, all of which challenged the perspective and authority of the religious leaders. These included the parable of the two sons, the parable of the wicked tenants, and the parable of the wedding feast.

On this day, it became clear to these religious leaders that if Jesus continued His ministry, there would be no place for them. He was exposing the emptiness of their hearts.

Today, we praise God that He has extended the invitation to the kingdom of heaven to all nations, all tribes, and all tongues – everyone! All He requires of us is our faith and our trust in Him.

Lord, we seek to follow You in Your suffering and in Your glory. Oh, that You would find us faithful in claiming Your authority as we bear witness to You in this fallen world. "And all things you ask in prayer, believing, you shall receive." This is the promise of God to us.

> **Within the Scripture, we read of the tension that begins to rise as Jesus continues to teach while His authority is questioned. What can we learn from the perseverance Jesus displays in this text?**

SONG FOR TODAY

"HALLELUJAH! WHAT A SAVIOR!"
Rowland Pritchard

Jesus! what a Friend for sinners!
Jesus! Lover of my soul;
Friends may fail me, foes assail me,
He, my Savior, makes me whole.
Hallelujah! What a Savior!
Hallelujah! What a Friend!

DAY 31

WEDNESDAY

MATTHEW 26:3-5; MARK 14:1-2; LUKE 21:37-38; LUKE 22:1-2

As followers of Jesus Christ, we believe and agree that the events and circumstances of this final week of Jesus' ministry are the most important of all human history. As we reach the midpoint of this Holy Week, and Jesus prepares for Passover, we observe Him maintaining His purpose with steadfastness and resolve. This last week of His life, He could be found teaching in the temple, investing in the lives of His followers, breathing out words of life, and retreating with His Father.

Certainly, the crowds grew exponentially to gather at the temple to hear Jesus. Rumors of His turning over tables and quieting the church leaders had likely made their way through Jerusalem and beyond. These followers, onlookers and enemies, would soon exchange their listening ears for shouts of "Crucify Him!" Jesus knew the cup that would be offered Him in the days to come, yet He continued to do His Father's work. O what a Savior!

Behind the scenes, religious leaders, chief priests and scribes were scheming hard. They wanted Jesus dead, but they were afraid of the crowds. As He gained followers, the ones who were most frightened by His popularity were those whose position He threatened.

But in God's divine providence, He was setting the table for the greatest moment ever in human history.

Jesus knew the cup He was to drink only days later, yet He continued to live His life in total obedience to His Father. He poured Himself out each day until His final breath, all the while, knowing the scheming and plotting that was happening behind the city gates. That next Passover celebration would see the final Lamb given in exchange for the sins of the world. Jesus was coming to the end of His life on this earth, and the church leaders and those in authority could not thwart what God had designed from the beginning of time.

Jesus never wavered in His calling, even to the point of His death. From the temple steps today, you can look across the city and see the Mount of Olives. The Garden of Gethsemane is located just below the Mount of Olives. And from both places, you can clearly see the temple. Jesus could see the soldiers and religious leaders coming in the night with their torches. And He waited, patiently waited, to offer up Himself for you and for me. O what a Savior!

As we meditate on the life of Christ, His final week, let us see Him as One who never wasted a moment to bring glory to His Father. Nothing is mundane or unimportant.

What a privilege it is to know God through Jesus Christ – the perfect, Lamb of God. O what a Savior!

Would you be able to trust God, knowing the outcome leads to your dying on a cross?
What is your response to the obedience Jesus displays in the days leading to His Crucifixion?

SONG FOR TODAY

"HOW DEEP THE FATHER'S LOVE"
Stuart Townend

DAY 32

THURSDAY

MATTHEW 26:17-46; MARK 14:12-23; 14:26-42; LUKE 22:7-46; JOHN 13:1-17:26

As the Jewish people look forward to the feast of Passover this evening, Jesus spends intentional time with His disciples, knowing that the time of His Crucifixion is fast approaching. Passover is a time to commemorate and celebrate how God delivered the Jewish people from Egypt. This Passover meal with Jesus and His disciples, however, would be particularly important and unique.

During this meal, Jesus communicates to His disciples that He is the one true Lamb. He breaks bread and shares it with His disciples. The unleavened bread symbolizes His body that will be broken on the Cross, and the cup they share symbolizes His blood that will be shed for the forgiveness of sins. Jesus institutes this practice, the Lord's Supper, as a way for His followers to commemorate His sacrifice. This act of remembrance not only honors Jesus' suffering on the Cross, but also points forward to His return.

While eating, Jesus astonishes His disciples by washing their feet. Although He is the Son of the Most High God, He humbles Himself to the lowest possible position and chooses to serve them rather than be served. In this act of service, Jesus models to His disciples ... and all followers ... how to serve and love others.

Judas, the disciple who will commit the most heinous act of betrayal, sits next to Jesus at the table. Jesus prophesies the coming betrayal, but the other disciples cannot believe this shocking revelation. Jesus also predicts He will be denied three times by Peter, one of His closest disciples. Peter, however, doesn't deem this possible because of his devotion to Jesus.

In both situations, Jesus demonstrates His sovereignty and supreme love. He knows what these men will do, but He does not reject them. The love drawing Him to the Cross extends to His most trusted followers even as they desert Him in His time of greatest need.

After the Passover meal, Jesus enters the Garden of Gethsemane to pray. He takes Peter, James and John with Him and commands them to watch and pray as He prepares for His Crucifixion. Instead, He returns to find them asleep. Jesus doesn't respond in anger but responds with grace. He continues to pray for the strength to submit Himself to the will of the Father.

On this same day, as recorded in John 13:34, Jesus commanded His followers to love one another as He has loved us. Each of this day's events is an example of how Jesus loved others even when He wasn't loved in return.

As you reflect on today's events, pray for humility, a greater dependence upon the Lord, and a passion to reach those who don't know Him as Savior.

> **Who comes to mind when you think about "loving those around us"? Take time to write their names down. How can you help them? How can you pray for them?**

SONG FOR TODAY

"IT IS WELL"

My sin, oh the bliss of this glorious thought
My sin, not in part, but the whole
Is nailed to the cross, and I bear it no more
Praise the Lord, praise the Lord, O my soul

DAY 33

GOOD FRIDAY

MATTHEW 26:47-27:61; MARK 14:43-15:47; LUKE 22:47-23:56;
JOHN 18:2-12; 15-18; 25-19:42

We are living in desperate and unprecedented times. And many wonder, where is God?

As we examine the last week in the life of Jesus, we have our answer. On Good Friday – He is on the Cross.

Christ's unbearable death was a sacrifice so that we could receive the unearned gift of eternal life. There was no other way.

The first Good Friday unfolds with Jesus' praying in Gethsemane, knowing what is to come: "My Father, if it be possible, let this cup pass from me; nevertheless, not as I will, but as you will." After the betrayal by Judas that leads to the arrest of the Messiah, Jesus acknowledges that "all this has taken place that the Scriptures of the prophets might be fulfilled."

After his arrest, Jesus faces false accusations from Jewish authorities during three stages of their religious court. Unlawful for them to put Jesus to death, they hand Him over to the Roman governor, Pilate. While Jesus suffers at the hands of Jewish leaders, His disciples experience their own torment – Simon Peter denies Jesus three times and Judas hangs himself.

Jesus faces three other stages in the Roman court. Although Pilate finds no wrongdoing, even symbolically washes his hands of the matter, he finally relents to pressure to crucify Jesus.

Roman soldiers scourge Jesus, beating Him nearly to the point of death. They mock His claim of being the Messiah – stripping Him of His clothes, covering Him with a purple cloak, and pounding a crown of thorns upon His head.

On the march to Golgotha, Jesus struggles to carry the heavy wooden cross on which He will die. An innocent bystander, Simon of Cyrene, helps when Jesus can barely stand.

Soldiers nail Jesus to the Cross, placing an inscription reading "The King of the Jews." And hours into the extreme torture of crucifixion, as He hangs between two criminals, Jesus cries out, "Father, into your hands I commit my spirit!" And he breathes his last breath.

Consider that somber yet powerful and magnificent moment under darkened skies: the earth trembles, rocks split, the huge temple veil tears in two, and tombs break open! Jesus accomplishes what He was supposed to for us. Lowered from the Cross, He is wrapped in fine linens and buried in a tomb – awaiting the Resurrection, His triumph over death.

As we contemplate the suffering of our Christ on this Good Friday, let us remember that we are never alone in our own suffering. No matter how dark and desperate life becomes, Jesus is there.

We must share how Jesus endured all those hours ... yet looked ahead to what was to come – something so beautiful, so glorious. Because for believers in Christ Jesus, there may be pain in the night, but joy comes in the morning.

We reflect on Good Friday knowing that Easter is coming.

> **Put yourself there with Jesus. Looking up at Him as He carries the weight of all sin and suffering. What would your response be, and how does it differ from your response now, knowing the story isn't over.**

SONG FOR TODAY

"THANK YOU, JESUS, FOR THE BLOOD"
Charity Gayle

FAITH IN PRACTICE

SILENT SATURDAY

MATTHEW 27:62-66

It was a dark and difficult day for the followers and friends of Jesus. Their Master, Lord and friend had just suffered the cruelest of deaths. He was now buried, and through earthly eyes, all hope seemed to have ended. Although He had explained the Father's plan, could they fully grasp it? Their journey with Him, as they had known, was finished.

Jesus had poured into them, demonstrating His love and power time and time again. The Father's plan was being fulfilled. Now, He was dead.

As we read in today's verses, the chief priests and Pharisees still believed Jesus had deceived the people. Jesus claimed to be the Son of God. Blasphemy! The people were still clueless about who Jesus really was. They implored Pilate to secure the tomb, and Pilate sent soldiers to carry out their wish. The tomb was sealed to prevent the disciples from stealing the body and claiming that Jesus had risen from the dead, making for an even worse deception. They were determined to put an end to this man, Jesus, who had offended them, challenged their laws, beliefs and practices. Now, they could rest peacefully, knowing He was dead and securely buried!

We are living in chaotic times and our faith is being challenged like never before.

Although we know God has a plan and is completely trustworthy, we sometimes find ourselves taking matters into our own hands. We worry, fret, and get overly stressed trying to determine how we will survive difficult days.

Unlike the disciples and others, we know the rest of the story. We know Jesus was victorious over death and is alive and well. We know from Scripture and from life experiences, God is sovereign and still on His throne. First John 4:4 reminds us, "… greater is He who is in you than he who is in the world."

We can draw strength and gain courage knowing firsthand that God is faithful. He is our refuge and strength, our ever-present help in times of trouble. These are troubling times, but with God's help and our constant abiding hope and faith properly placed in Him, the Church will not only survive this time but thrive during it!

Pray, asking God to give you a teachable spirit to learn what it is He has for you during these difficult days. Press into Him and allow Him to have His way in your life as you simply trust and follow our risen Lord, day by day.

DAY 34

MARK 15:46

And Joseph bought a linen shroud, and taking him down, wrapped him in the linen shroud and laid him in a tomb that had been cut out of the rock. And he rolled a stone against the entrance of the tomb.

On this day, the body of Jesus was laid in a sealed tomb with guards standing watch. Silence fell on the hearts of those who stood with tears in their eyes, wondering ... was it over? Within the silence, faith is tested, patience can be broken, and fears can be born. If we were to take time to reflect on our lives, we would all find moments where the silence brought forth thoughts of doubt, but the truth is that in seasons of silence, His grace speaks louder. Today let's turn our moments of silence into intentional moments of deeper prayer and reflection on the power and beauty displayed within this powerful story.

Today let's challenge ourselves not to run from the silence but meditate within it. We must listen to the words He is speaking, holding fast, knowing He isn't finished, and fall deeper in love with His redemptive story. Now go and utilize the silence that today brings.

Scan the QR code to experience the fullness of these devotionals by listening to the worship songs complementing them.

DAY 35

EASTER SUNDAY

MATTHEW 28:1-10; MARK 16:1-7; LUKE 24:1-43; JOHN 20:1-23

Imagine that Sunday morning. The women looking for the body of Jesus are confused and frustrated. When a young man in a white robe speaks to them, they are afraid and flee from the tomb. Later, the disciples hear that the tomb holding Jesus is empty. Peter runs to the tomb, and then returns home, marveling at what happened.

Two followers of Jesus walking on the road to Emmaus talk about the news they heard from Jerusalem when they are joined by Jesus. They do not recognize Him until He breaks bread in front of them. More begin hearing that Jesus is alive. He appears to most of the disciples and shows them His hands and His side. Thomas is not with them and does not believe until he is able to see Jesus.

Although we know the rest of the story, they do not. They have trouble understanding the Resurrection. They had seen Jesus demonstrate His power over nature. They had seen Jesus demonstrate His power over disease, and even death. But now they must believe that He even had power over His *own* death. That morning changed their world ... and ours.

The Resurrection of Jesus is the pivotal event in human history. Jesus predicted His Resurrection when He proclaimed to the religious leaders, "Destroy this temple, and I will raise it up again in three days." He not only appeared to hundreds of people, He also spent 40 days with the disciples, traveling and teaching.

The Resurrection of Jesus is the foundation of our Christian faith. Paul reminds us, "For as by a man came death, by a man has come also the resurrection of the dead." Paul also teaches that belief in the Resurrection is a foundational element of our salvation: "If you confess with your mouth that Jesus is Lord and believe in your heart that God raised Him from the dead, you will be saved."

The Resurrection of Jesus also proclaims victory over death. Death is not the end; instead, death is the final enemy to be destroyed. Paul asks, "O death, where is your victory? O death, where is your sting?" That is why he can boldly state: "For to me, to live is Christ, and to die is gain."

On this Resurrection Day, we sing "Christ the Lord is risen today." The Resurrection of Jesus is the foundation of our faith. The Resurrection of Jesus is the basis for our salvation. And the Resurrection of Jesus demonstrates His victory over death and our sure hope of eternal life.

> **The Resurrection of Jesus is the pivotal moment in human history. Take time to reflect and write how this great display of love has forever changed your life.**

SONG FOR TODAY

"WHEN I SURVEY THE WONDROUS CROSS"

When I survey the wondrous cross
On which the Prince of glory died
My richest gain I count but loss
And pour contempt on all my pride

HE IS NOT HERE, FOR HE HAS

MATTHEW 28:6

Published by Prestonwood Baptist Church
Copyright ©2023 by Prestonwood Baptist Church

All rights reserved. No part of this book may be reproduced in any form.

All Scripture verses quoted are used with permission:

The Holy Bible, English Standard Version® (ESV®)
Copyright © 2001 by Crossway, a publishing ministry of Good News Publishers.
All rights reserved. The ESV text may not be quoted in any publication made available to
the public by a Creative Commons license. The ESV may not be translated in whole
or in part into any other language.

ESV Text Edition: 2016
The Holy Bible, English Standard Version (ESV) is adapted from the Revised Standard
Version of the Bible, copyright Division of Christian Education of the National Council of the
Churches of Christ in the U.S.A. All rights reserved.

Crossway is a not-for-profit organization (a publishing ministry of Good News Publishers)
that exists solely for the purpose of publishing the good news of the gospel and the truth
of God's Word, the Bible. A portion of the purchase price of every Bible is donated to
help support Bible distribution ministry around the world.

For more information:
Prestonwood Baptist Church
6801 W. Park Blvd.
Plano, Texas 75093

prestonwood.org

Jesus is the King of Kings and the Lord of Lords, and we celebrate His grace, His goodness, His greatness and His glory on our road to Easter, on Resurrection Sunday and every day!

Not only did Jesus die on the Cross for our sins, but He also rose again! He conquered death for us, and we are blessed to celebrate the miraculous event of His Resurrection. We live with confidence and security because we have a sure hope in Him.

In *Living Hope: A Devotional for The Church, by The Church*, you will take a five-week journey, front and center, into the powerful story of the Crucifixion and Resurrection of Jesus Christ – our "living hope."

The first four weeks of the book will strengthen your heart, soul and mind by working through a different spiritual discipline each week. Those disciplines will set the table for week five – Holy Week. Our goal is to help you put your faith into practice, preparing your heart for the powerful story displayed throughout Holy Week. Within the pages of this book, your days will consist of either a "Daily Devotional" or a "Faith in Practice." To complement your daily readings, you will find music interwoven throughout the book, bringing a beautiful parallel for this special time of worship, meditation and reflection.

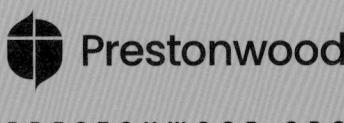